GREAT WESTERN BRANCH LINES

1 – The South West

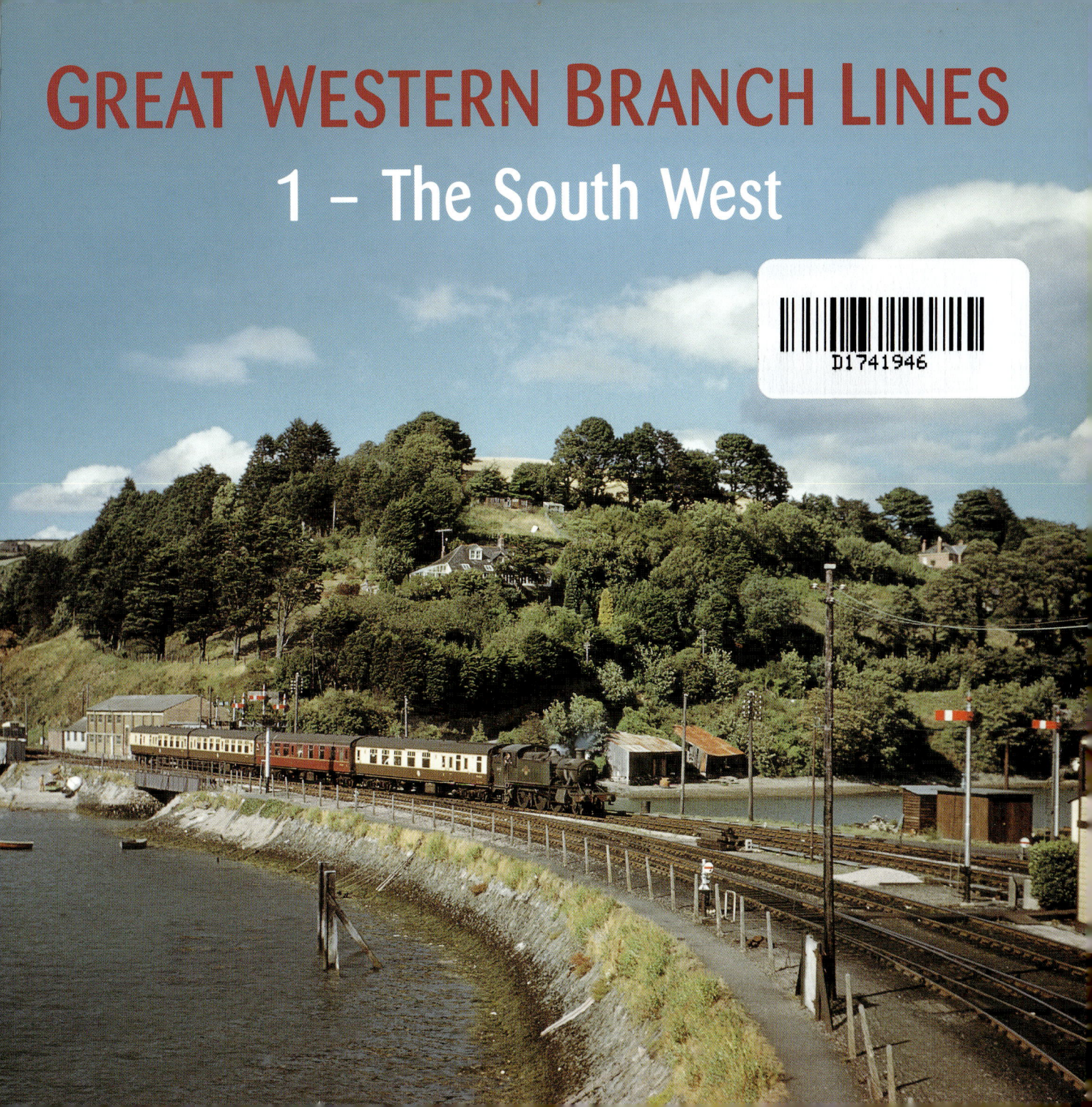

© Michael S Welch 2002
Published by Runpast Publishing, 10 Kingscote Grove, Cheltenham, Gloucestershire GL51 6JX.

ISBN 1 870754 54 9

Typesetting and reproduction by Viners Wood Associates. Printed in England by Colorworks.

A peaceful scene at Newent, on the former Gloucester to Ledbury line, a truly rural branch which served no intermediate significant centres of population. Needless to say, the train is a special organised by a local railway society, motive power being 0-6-0PT No.6424, which had obviously been spruced up for the occasion: this picture was taken on 23rd June 1962. By this date the branch had already been closed to passengers for almost three years, but the section south of Dymock remained open for freight, though even this ceased in 1964 when the branch passed into history.

Roy Denison

Introduction

The Great Western Railway (GWR) was known to its many devotees as 'God's Wonderful Railway' while its detractors often referred to it disparagingly as the 'Great Way Round'. Love it or loathe it, there was no doubt that the GWR played a key role in the history of Britain's railway system and made a huge impact on the industrial and social development of the nation.

This book is not concerned with these weighty matters however, but focuses on a comparatively small area of the GWR's operations. In this album I have sought to convey something of the atmosphere of GWR branch and secondary lines in the south west of England which, for the purposes of this book, is defined as stretching from Gloucestershire to Cornwall. Many of these routes were conceived by local people who merely desired to see the town in which they lived connected to the expanding railway system, thus enabling passengers and goods to be moved much more speedily and efficiently than hitherto. Needless to say in the vast majority of cases they struggled to raise the necessary finance and frequently one of the established companies, such as the Bristol & Exeter Railway, which had the necessary financial muscle and engineering expertise, would have to rescue them. Some of the lines, such as the Taunton to Chard branch in Somerset, were built to the broad gauge, while others like the Chacewater to Newquay byway, in total contrast, arrived on the scene long after broad gauge had been abandoned! By the end of the 19th century the GWR had swallowed up many smaller companies and the uniform nature of the operation had become firmly established. The system was operated by a distinctive family of locomotives, while standardised designs of rolling stock, signalling equipment and structures combined to give the GWR an extremely recognisable identity. It certainly didn't need a trade mark. Everybody soon learned how easy it was to distinguish the GWR from other companies.

The GWR always tried to cater for the local communities it served and enterprisingly pioneered the steam railmotor which first appeared on the Stonehouse to Chalford line in 1903. These generated much additional traffic, but suffered from an inherent problem – they were inflexible and unable to power additional coaches. The railmotors were superceded by auto trains, a push-pull operation with a separate locomotive and coaches, which did not have the railmotor's drawbacks. The engines which were most prominent on the GWR's auto train services were 1400 Class 0-4-2Ts, 4575 Class 2-6-2Ts and some pannier tanks and the pictures which follow reflect their dominance. Another development was the opening of many halts during the inter-war period, and frequently these had the characteristic 'pagoda' type waiting shelter with a short, wooden-edged platform. Camping coaches, which were located at especially picturesque spots in the countryside or beside the sea, were a colourful feature of some stations, Gara Bridge and Blue Anchor being particular examples. The GWR would sometimes 'landscape' stations with trees, shrubs and flowerbeds and even today, long after the closure of a line and demolition of stations, GWR pine trees can still be seen, marking the location where a station once stood. The 1920s and 1930s saw increased competition from road transport and the GWR fought this challenge by introducing its own network of buses which fed rural railheads and complemented its rail routes. However, some lines covered by this volume

retained their individual characteristics, notably the MSWJR which remained independent until 1923 and even afterwards retained a close-knit family atmosphere, until it succumbed to closure in 1961. Another exception was the Hemyock branch, a real gem if ever there was one, which was built as the Culm Valley Light Railway in 1876. Passenger traffic lasted until September 1963, while the line's milk traffic sustained it until total closure in November 1975.

Following the Second World War the growth of road transport heralded the decline of many branch and secondary routes. Some, such as the Princetown and Moretonhampstead lines, served thinly populated areas, and it is unlikely they ever paid their way. These succumbed to closure to passenger traffic in the 1950s, long before the late Doctor (later Lord) Beeching started to wield his dreaded axe. Another development, widely extended in the post-war era, was paid holidays and these led to a massive upsurge in week-end travel during the summer months. Naturally, with its glorious scenery, attractive resorts and agreeable climate, the West Country was a hugely popular destination and most visitors arrived by rail. Summer Saturdays on the principal routes to the west in the 1950s were very busy, and this increase in holiday traffic naturally affected the secondary routes. Those such as the Taunton to Barnstaple line, which only had a local Monday to Friday passenger service, were suddenly transformed on summer Saturdays into main holiday routes. On the Newquay line, for example, through services were provided for holiday-makers to London and the Midlands and they were invariably heavy trains, sometimes double-headed over the branch's steep inclines. It was not unknown for 'Castle' Class locomotives to work to Newquay, where they were never seen during the quiet winter months. But the harsh economic realities of the 1960s spelt doom for many West Country lines, some of which may never have been a paying proposition at any time during their careers and, sadly, most had been removed from the railway map by the end of that decade. A glance at a Western Region early 1960s timetable will reveal the sparse service advertised on many branches, which reflected the rural nature of the areas they served. It was a pity, however, that so little appears to have been done to publicise their scenic attractions and run the lines more economically – certainly a wasted opportunity. But all is not completely lost, because some lines still operate as part of the national system, especially in Cornwall, and others have become tourist railways run by enthusiasts. It is still possible, therefore, for readers to relive, or perhaps experience for the first time, some of the magical, unique flavour of a GWR West Country branch line.

During this compilation I have received considerable assistance from many people. Firstly, I would like to thank the many photographers who trusted me with their irreplaceable colour transparencies, without whose help the completion of this volume would have been impossible. In addition, Alan Bennett, Roy Denison, David Fakes and Graham Mallinson have kindly scrutinised the manuscript and suggested innummerable corrections and improvements, although I accept responsibility for any errors which have slipped through.

M. S. W. Burgess Hill, West Sussex, April 2002

Gloucester to Ledbury

The 19 miles-long Gloucester to Ledbury line was one of a number of picturesque secondary lines that radiated from Gloucester. It started as two separate locally promoted schemes, the Newent Railway and the Ross & Ledbury Railway, both of which were authorised by Acts of Parliament in 1873. The GWR provided the necessary funds however, and construction commenced in 1881 with the line opening to traffic on 27th July 1885. Remarkably, the section from Ledbury to Dymock was built as a double track line, while the stretch south of Dymock was single track. The former section was singled in 1907. Some of the route was laid on the course of the Herefordshire & Gloucestershire Canal, part of which dated from 1798. The passenger service on this predominantly rural route remained fairly static during the entire history of the line – just five trains each way on weekdays. In later years the line was largely operated by GWR diesel railcars, but despite the economies these introduced it was still deemed to be 'unremunerative', and BR withdrew the passenger service from 13th July 1959. The section north of Dymock shut completely, but the line from Over Junction (Gloucester) to Dymock was retained for goods traffic until 1964. This presented opportunities for railtours, and one of these trains is seen at Barber's Bridge with 6400 Class locomotive No.6424 on 23rd June 1962. Note that the running-in board is still *in situ* almost three years after closure to passengers!

Roy Denison

Gloucester to Hereford

A splendid picture of Mitcheldean Road station, which was presumably taken from the top of a signal post, showing the idyllic setting of this pretty station. This shot was taken in June 1962. The author could not resist including this photograph, but strictly speaking it does not qualify for inclusion in this album because the station is located just over a mile across the county border in Herefordshire, but it is more than likely that some of the distant hills are in Gloucestershire.

Roy Denison

A scene at Longhope, photographed on 3rd November 1962, showing Collett-designed 2251 Class 0-6-0 No.2242 engaging in a little light shunting. The train is a Hereford to Gloucester freight, commonly known as a 'pick-up', which stopped as required at wayside stations to detach or collect wagons – the type of train hardly ever seen on today's railway system. The delightful autumn colours of the lineside trees will be noted. No.2242 appears to have a very severely burnt smokebox door, doubtless the result of it not sealing properly and drawing air. On 31st October 1964 the late Doctor (later Lord) Beeching's wretched axe struck a number of WR passenger services, including the Gloucester to Hereford line, which at that time had eight weekday return passenger workings. Freight services from Gloucester continued to Ross-on-Wye and to Lydbrook Junction, on the Monmouth line, for another year.

Roy Denison

Oakle Street station was located between Gloucester and Grange Court Junction, where the Hereford branch diverged from the main line to South Wales. The station only served a small hamlet of a few cottages which was situated west of the station. Here a very grimy Churchward-designed 4300 Class 'Mogul', No.6349, is seen departing from Oakle Street with the 2.30pm train from Gloucester to Hereford on 9th May 1964. The highly scenic line to Hereford was originally built as a single-track broad gauge route and opened as the Hereford, Ross and Gloucester Railway on 1st June 1855, though the GWR worked the line from the outset. It was converted to standard gauge in 1866, an operation which apparently took a mere five days to complete. Interestingly, the line's passenger trains remained wholly steam-worked until closure. *Alan Chandler*

The Cinderford Branch

Left, above: A shot of the Railway Enthusiasts Club 'Severn Boar' brake van special, taken in June 1964, depicting 1600 Class 0-6-0PT No.1658 climbing towards Cinderford, in the Forest of Dean. The train is seen between Soudley and Ruspidge halts. At one time this line had a passenger service which operated from Newnham, on the Lydney to Gloucester route, to Cinderford and on to Drybrook, a distance of 8¼ miles. The service was initially worked by railmotors which served numerous tiny halts *en route*. The section beyond Cinderford lasted until 7th July 1930, while passenger services on the lower stretch of the line were withdrawn by BR on 3rd November 1958.   *Roy Hobbs*

Lydney to Sharpness

Left, below: A fine panoramic view of the former bridge across the River Severn at Sharpness, taken on the same day as the previous picture, with the REC brake van special standing in the ruins of the abandoned Severn Bridge station. This line was formerly part of the Severn & Wye Joint Railway which was operated by the GWR and Midland companies. Latterly an auto-train service was provided across the bridge linking Lydney Town and Berkeley Road stations, but on the night of 25th October 1960 two barges collided with one of the piers in thick fog, demolishing two spans. Initially, there was considerable local optimism that the bridge, a marvel of Victorian engineering, would be rebuilt, but this proved to be unfounded and it was eventually demolished. Passenger traffic continued on the surviving rump of the line, from Berkeley Road to Sharpness, for some years afterwards, but the route no longer fulfilled its original purpose and patronage dwindled away with the result that the last passenger trains ran on 31st October 1964. Note the track of the Lydney to Gloucester line which is just visible in front of the trees on the right.   *Roy Hobbs*

Cheltenham to Kingham

On a beautiful October day in 1955, 4575 Class 2-6-2T No.5518 is seen leaving Andoversford with a local train to Kingham. The attractive carmine and cream livery of the coaches stands out in this shot. Andoversford was the junction between the Midland & South Western Junction Railway's (MSWJR) line to Cirencester, Swindon and Andover, the tracks of which are in the foreground, and the GWR's Cheltenham to Kingham route. The former route was deliberately run down by BR, and prior to closure only one train in each direction ran on weekdays between Andoversford and Cirencester, although the service south from there was a little more generous. The much lamented MSWJR line was closed to passengers in September 1961. The line to Kingham had six return trains each weekday and lasted a little longer, not succumbing until October 1962.

S. C. Townroe/Colour-Rail

Gloucester to Chalford

It is debatable whether the Chalford auto service qualifies for inclusion in this album because it ran along the important Gloucester to Swindon line which has through main line services to Paddington. The Gloucester to Chalford auto trains were very similar in character to a branch line operation however, latterly usually employing 1400 Class 0-4-2Ts on a couple of coaches. A steam railmotor, which stopped at tiny halts to serve small settlements, was inaugurated by the GWR on this section in 1903 and was later introduced in other areas. The Gloucester Central to Chalford trains served no fewer than twelve stations in sixteen miles, including Stroud, which was the principal town on the line. In this picture a rather dirty 1400 Class locomotive, No.1445, heads up the Golden Valley near Stroud with the 4.40pm Stonehouse (Burdett Road) to Brimscombe train on 9th May 1964. This was presumably a 'rush hour' service provided especially for homegoing workers. *Alan Chandler*

The smoke being emitted by 1400 Class 0-4-2T No.1472, seen here at Ham Mill Halt propelling a Chalford to Gloucester working, does its best to ruin the superb view down the Golden Valley towards Stroud. The halt's simple construction is evident in this view, but at least a shelter was provided for passengers which was, perhaps, more than the local bus stop offered! Some of the halts on the line boasted distinctive corrugated iron sheeted 'pagoda' style shelters. The locomotive's fireman will be able to relax on this trip, the line to Gloucester being downhill virtually all of the way. This photograph was taken on 6th April 1963.

Roy Denison

When the line up the Stroud Valley was being planned, Brunel wanted to use a different route with easier gradients. Unfortunately, there was a pressing need to save money on construction costs and the present course was adopted, despite its long and tortuous climb, some of which is on a gradient of 1 in 60, towards Sapperton Tunnel. Generations of enginemen probably complained bitterly about this decision, because it presented heavy trains with a formidable obstacle, and in steam days a banking engine was usually available at Brimscombe to assist as required. The 1400 Class 0-4-2Ts did not completely monopolise the local auto train passenger service up the valley, and in this shot 0-6-0PT No.3775 is depicted near Brimscombe Bridge Halt hauling a Chalford-bound train in June 1964. Between those two points the line steepens considerably but, hopefully, the crew of No.3775 were able to reach their destination without the services of a 'banker'! Sadly, despite being well patronised this useful service was withdrawn in October 1964 and all of the small halts were closed.

Roy Hobbs

Fairford station

The 25½ miles-long line from Oxford to Fairford was opened in two sections which were originally proposed by separate local companies. The Oxford to Witney stretch was opened by the Witney Railway amidst much local celebration on 13th November 1861. The remaining part of the branch was built by the East Gloucestershire Railway (EGR) and opened on 15th June 1873. This company had grand ideas to run through services from Cheltenham to Faringdon with a branch to Witney, and Fairford station, which was situated on the fringe of the town, was built with through running in mind. Apart from construction of the Fairford to Witney section, predictably perhaps, nothing further came of the EGR's grandiose plans and in 1890 the GWR absorbed both the EGR and the Witney Railway. Around half a

dozen weekday trains were generally provided, with a journey along the entire line taking 70 minutes. Perhaps the heyday of this sleepy branch line was during the Second World War when considerable freight traffic to various airfields in the area justified 24 hours a day operation. On the passenger side a new station was commissioned at Carterton to serve the large Brize Norton airfield, and an additional daily train provided. Despite local opposition, passenger traffic ceased from 18th June 1962, the section beyond Witney being closed to all traffic. In this picture 0-6-0PT No.3653 is seen at Fairford after arrival with the 1.44pm from Oxford on 19th May 1962. The line continued beyond the station for a short distance to the goods yard and small engine shed.

Neville Simms

Cirencester Town station

There were two stations at Cirencester, one on the MSWJR's Cheltenham to Swindon line, which was latterly known as Cirencester Watermoor, the other being Cirencester Town. The latter was included in an Act of 1836 which authorised the much larger scheme for a line between Swindon and Gloucester (Standish Junction). The route from Swindon to Cirencester Town opened on 31st May 1841 as a broad gauge line, before the line to Standish Junction had been completed. When that opened to traffic a local landowner objected to a station being built at the branch's junction with (what had become) the main line, so passengers had to use a 'temporary' wooden exchange-only platform until a 'proper' station could be provided. This ridiculous state of affairs continued for more than forty years, until Kemble station opened on 1st May 1882. In the meantime the Cirencester branch was converted to standard gauge in May 1872. One of the branch's claims to fame was that just outside Kemble it crossed over the infant waters of the River Thames a little over a mile from its source. Steam operated passenger trains were replaced by diesel railbuses in February 1959 in an attempt to improve the branch's viability. A number of tiny wooden halts was also opened at the same time, hopefully to increase passenger numbers. These measures were obviously not successful however, passenger trains being withdrawn from 6th April 1964 and goods traffic eighteen months later. Cirencester Town station's lovely, ornate Gothic-style station building is seen in this view. This main building is the original, dating from the line's opening in 1841, though the gentlemen's toilet appears to be a later addition.   *Roy Denison*

The Malmesbury Branch

Right, above: The 6½ miles-long line from Dauntsey to Malmesbury was promoted by a local company which obtained an Act on 25th July 1872. The 'locals' only managed to raise a proportion of the money required, so the branch was constructed in partnership with the GWR. There was only one wayside station on the line, at Somerford 2¾ miles from Dauntsey, this station being renamed Great Somerford in 1903. The branch opened amidst much local celebration on 17th December 1877, a public holiday being proclaimed in Malmesbury. What better way of advertising the new railway could there have been? The initial service was six trains each way on weekdays, with extra workings on market days. In 1903 a new, direct route from Swindon to South Wales was opened by the GWR and this crossed the branch by means of a bridge just north of Great Somerford. In 1933 the GWR installed a spur from Little Somerford, on the 'new' main line, which shortened the branch to 3¾ miles, and therefore economised on operating costs. The line south thereof to Dauntsey was then abandoned. The passenger service lasted until 8th September 1951 – the GWR's 'new' connection was obviously not enough to stave off closure. In this shot, 5800 Class 0-4-2T No.5802 enters Malmesbury station with an enthusiasts' special on 18th August 1957. The landmark on the right of the picture is the ancient Malmesbury Abbey which overlooks the town from a hilltop. *Trevor Owen*

Right, below: Despite its relatively early closure to passenger trains, the Malmesbury branch remained open for goods traffic until 11th November 1962, the final train apparently being powered by 204hp 0-6-0 diesel shunter No.D2196. After the passenger workings ceased most of the structures at the terminus remained intact, and in this illustration, also taken on 18th August 1957, the neat station, rather ramshackle engine shed and water tower can be seen. The train in the platform is the rear of the railtour depicted in the previous picture.

Trevor Owen

Avoncliff Halt

Left, above: Avoncliff Halt, looking westwards on 5th May 1963. The bridge is actually an aqueduct which carries the Kennet & Avon Canal across the railway: note that each track has a separate arch. This tiny halt, which serves a small hamlet, probably owes its continued existence to the steep roads and narrow lanes in the area, which presumably prevent easy access by buses. The section between Trowbridge and Bathampton (on the London to Bath main line) was the subject of considerable controversy and legal wrangles in the 1850s due to the failure of the Wiltshire, Somerset & Weymouth Railway company to complete the line as stipulated in their original 1845 Act. This company was absorbed by the GWR in 1850, and legal proceedings were taken against the GWR in an attempt to force them to finish the line. This action was successful, the route eventually opening on 2nd February 1857. A single broad gauge track was laid, but the line was converted to standard gauge in June 1874, and later doubled in 1885 as a result of increasing coal traffic between South Wales and Southampton.
Roy Denison

Left, below: A down freight train from Westbury is depicted passing Avoncliff Halt, between Bradford-on-Avon and Bath, behind pannier tank No.9632 in September 1962. This halt, which is still open for business, is delightfully situated in the Avon valley 1½ miles west of Bradford-on-Avon. The frequency of trains on the Salisbury to Bristol route was reasonably generous, but Avoncliff Halt, as might be expected, had the worst service of any station on the line. In the summer 1961 timetable about eight trains were booked to call in each direction on Mondays to Fridays, the service clearly being designed primarily for morning rush hour travellers to Bath and Bristol, and returning passengers in the evening. The off-peak service was extremely sparse.
P. A. Fry/Colour-Rail

Cheltenham to Andover

Foss Cross was a little-known and remote station on the northern section of the Midland & South Western Junction Railway between Cheltenham and Cirencester. The station served a tiny hamlet which is located at a nearby cross roads on Fosse Way, an ancient Roman road, hence the name. The first section of the MSWJR opened from Swindon to Marlborough in July 1881, this line being extended to Andover in February 1883. On 18th December 1883 an extension northwards from Swindon was opened for business as far as Cirencester. The final link on to Cheltenham, which included the station seen here, was not completed until 30th June 1891. The route through the Cotswold hills via Foss Cross was built as single track but some sections were subsequently converted to double track, only to be singled by the GWR in the 1920s. The MSWJR was independent of the GWR until the Grouping in 1923 and this, together with the line's relative isolation, ensured that it maintained a family atmosphere and distinctive character well into BR days. The last ordinary passenger trains between Cheltenham, Swindon and Andover ran on 9th/10th September 1961, but freight and some special passenger workings continued on parts of the MSWJ after this date. This shot was taken on 1st October 1961, a few weeks after closure. *Roy Denison*

17

A view of Swindon Town station on 21st August 1960, showing BR Standard Class 4MT 4-6-0 No.75029, in creditably clean condition, in the southbound platform at the head of an unidentified local working, possibly the 4.52pm to Andover Junction. The fortunes of the former MSWJR line had reached its nadir by the early 1960s, although Swindon Town station was relatively busy compared to others on the line. Three weekday trains to and from Andover were advertised in the summer 1961 timetable. The principal trains of the day were the 7.50am Andover to Cheltenham St. James, and its corresponding return working, the 1.52pm Cheltenham St. James to Southampton Terminus, which by this date had become the only trains to run north of Cirencester. In addition, one or two short workings operated to Marlborough, Cirencester and Chiseldon, so it could be said that Swindon Town was almost the 'hub' of the line! No.75029 was lucky enough to survive into preservation, being purchased upon withdrawal by the well-known artist David Shepherd. *Roy Denison*

Ogbourne station was situated about seven miles south of Swindon and served the village of Ogbourne St George. Prior to closure there were three southbound trains on weekdays to Andover, plus a lunchtime short working to Marlborough on Saturdays only. In the reverse direction three weekday services to Swindon Town were provided, with an extra lunchtime train on Saturdays. Withdrawal of the passenger service is unlikely to have caused much hardship to travellers from Ogbourne, the station being adjacent to the main Swindon to Marlborough road. This portrait was taken on 15th October 1961, a few weeks after services ceased and the station site has since been obliterated by a road scheme.   *Roy Denison*

Photographed against a distinctive background of downland, with a housing estate in the middle foreground, a two-coach local train to Swindon leaves Marlborough behind an unidentified GWR 0-6-0PT in the early 1960s. Judging by the fairly cloudy sky, the photographer appears to have been extremely fortunate to have had the sun shining just as the train passed his vantage point. *Roy Denison collection*

Right, above: A view of Marlborough station on 15th March 1958 showing a GWR-designed pannier tank locomotive, No.9672, on the front of an unidentified southbound passenger train pausing at the former MSWJR station. The GWR premises in the town closed to passengers as long ago as 6th March 1933. Note the refreshment room, which does not look particularly inviting, and the platform barrow, an item of station furniture which is hardly ever seen these days. The station is in rather scruffy condition, and brightened up only by the colourful posters for 'Party Outings by Rail' and 'Snowcem'. The station building could have done with a touch of the latter product! At the time of this photograph Marlborough still had a service of three weekday trains to Cheltenham, while five trains were advertised southwards to Andover. In addition a purely local service ran to Savernake (Low Level) station to connect with main line trains. *Trevor Owen*

Right, below: In this portrait, Marlborough station is seen on a sunny 14th October 1961, shortly after closure to regular passenger traffic, to which the rusty rails bear testament. The line was still open for freight and occasional special passenger trains run for pupils at Marlborough College. The stretch of wooded downland in the background is Postern Hill. This view was taken looking eastwards and the photographer was standing on the bridge that carried the line over the main Andover to Swindon road. Two last day specials traversed the line on 10th September 1961, a Railway Correspondence & Travel Society train from Swindon, hauled by 4300 Class 2-6-0 No.5306, and a Stephenson Locomotive Society excursion from Birmingham which was powered by GWR-designed 'Manor' Class 4-6-0 No.7808 *Cookham Manor*. *Roy Denison*

Around Devizes

In BR days the service to Devizes was unenterprising, and consisted mainly of a handful of semi-fast or stopping trains from Paddington or Newbury to Westbury or Bristol and vice versa. There were also a few purely local workings to either Patney & Chirton, for main line connections, or Westbury. One of the slowest trains (in the 1961 summer timetable) was the 7.5am from Paddington to Westbury, which stopped at all stations after Reading and reached Devizes, 86 miles from Paddington, at 9.58am! The train seen here pausing in Devizes station on 14th July 1962, is the 2.35pm Paddington to Weston-super-Mare, a semi-fast working, which covered the distance from London to the Wiltshire town in 2hrs. 10mins. – a much more respectable performance. Motive power is provided by 'Castle' Class 4-6-0 No.5072 *Hurricane*. The Devizes line provided a useful diversionary route from London to Bristol in emergency, but despite this it was closed completely in April 1966 when Devizes lost all rail connection. Loss of main line status at the turn of the century proved to be Devizes's downfall.

Roy Denison

In 1836 Brunel drew up plans for a line from Chippenham to Westbury which incorporated a branch to Devizes, but nothing came of the scheme. The next development occurred on 30th June 1845 when the Wiltshire, Somerset & Weymouth Railway, a nominally independent concern backed by the GWR, obtained Parliamentary consent for its line from Thingley Junction to Westbury together with branches to Devizes and Bradford-on-Avon. The Devizes branch opened for traffic on 1st July 1857 and the town was, after years of campaigning, on the railway map. This line did not satisfy the townfolk's desire for a direct connection to the Capital however, and pressure was brought to bear on the GWR who seemed indifferent to the demands. In the late 1850s a Berks. & Hants. Extension Railway was proposed, supported by the citizens of Devizes, and this broad gauge line from Hungerford opened on 11th November 1862, thus creating a through route. At last the town had a direct line to Paddington, and the townspeople expected it would also become the GWR's principal route to the West of England. In 1883 however the GWR obtained Parliamentary consent for a new, main line from Patney to Westbury, which avoided Devizes. The town's citizens were horrified and made representations to Parliament, but to no avail, the new route being opened in July 1900 and hopes that Devizes would have permanent main line status were dashed. In this picture, the Locomotive Club of Great Britain's 'Wessex Downsman' railtour is depicted passing Bromham & Rowde Halt, west of Devizes, behind 'Hall' Class 4-6-0 No.6963 *Throwley Hall en route* from Reading to Bristol on 4th April 1965. The train later travelled over the Somerset & Dorset line.

Trevor Owen

Chippenham to Calne

The 5¼ miles-long branch from Chippenham to Calne was incorporated under the Calne Railway Act of 15th May 1860 and the line was opened on the 3rd November 1863. It was a single track broad gauge route, but gauge conversion took place from 14th August 1874. The next milestones in the line's career occurred in July 1892 when the Calne Railway was absorbed by the GWR, and in 1895, when Calne station was rebuilt. The line boasted two intermediate halts, of which the first to be built, Black Dog Halt, was constructed in 1874 as a private halt for a local landowner who did not permit it to appear in the public timetable until the early 1950s. Stanley Bridge Halt, opened in April 1905, was a typical GWR wayside halt complete with a corrugated iron pagoda-style waiting shelter, oil lamps and

timber platform edging. Steam railmotors were used on the line until the 1930s, when they were superseded by auto trains usually worked by 1400 Class 0-4-2Ts. There was significant passenger business to and from local RAF stations and considerable goods traffic originating from a cooked meat factory at Calne. Latterly, the regular passenger trains had been formed of dmus and the final steam working to Calne reportedly occurred on 20th September 1964, this being a special powered by 1400 Class No.1444, which is pictured above. The last scheduled public passenger train, formed of a dmu, operated almost exactly a year afterwards, on 18th September 1965. The last post was sounded as it left Calne and on arrival at Chippenham, after which the branch faded into history.

Trevor Owen

Yeovil to Weymouth

Right, above: The Yeovil to Weymouth line, besides being an exceedingly pretty route through a thinly populated part of Dorset, is also extremely steeply graded with long climbs in each direction to a summit at Evershot tunnel. The ascent is steeper from Yeovil, with four miles varying in grade from 1 in 74 to 1 in 51 – quite a challenge. In this picture, taken on a scorching, hot June day in 1964, the fireman of Bulleid 'Battle of Britain' Pacific No.34057 *Biggin Hill* must have been working really hard as the train climbed towards the summit. Unfortunately from the photographer's point of view, it also appears that he was a master of his craft, as there is hardly a trace of smoke being emitted by No.34057, which indicates excellent combustion. But there does appear to be some smoke at the rear of the train ...
Roy Hobbs

Right, below: ... it is unlikely that even such a powerful locomotive as *Biggin Hill* would have 'made it' to the summit on the heavy ten coach train without some loss of time, so Yeovil shed thoughtfully provided a banking engine to assist. BR Standard Class 3MT 2-6-2T No.82044 was the locomotive selected for the job, and is seen here pushing mightily at the rear. Note the trap point installed at this location to deflect any runaway vehicles away from the running lines. On the last day of steam on the Southern Region, 9th July 1967, this route was unexpectedly traversed by a number of special 'perishable' trains which ran from Weymouth to Westbury and formed the largest contingent of SR steam-hauled workings on that fateful day. Ironically, these trains took the engines onto Western Region metals which had been devoid of steam traction for more than eighteen months.
Roy Hobbs

A portrait of Maiden Newton station, on the former GWR main line from Yeovil to Weymouth, taken on 20th September 1961. This station serves a village of the same name and is still in business today. This route was originally promoted by the Wiltshire, Somerset & Weymouth Railway under GWR auspices as a broad gauge line, and opened on 20th January 1857. In times gone by, it was a relatively busy line and until the late 1950s offered a through service to London Paddington. In more recent times the line has been singled, and downgraded in status to little more than a branch with only a sparse Weymouth to Bristol service. The picture is dominated by the substantial GWR signal box, but the signals themselves appear to be a mix of GWR and 'Southern' types. Note the broad gauge goods shed. The mixture of platform furniture will be noted, the Southern Railway concrete lamp posts contrasting with the GWR-style running-in board, which exhorts passengers to change for Bridport. The rather curious assortment of platform fittings and signalling equipment is no doubt a legacy of the 1950 to 1958 period when this part of the route was under Southern Region control.

John Langford

Bridport Branch

In this very rare colour picture of BR steam at Bridport, 0-6-0 pannier tank No.3759 is seen on a short goods working in the late 1950s. The Bridport branch was promoted locally by the Bridport Railway Company which was incorporated on 5th May 1855, and authorised to construct an 11¼ miles-long broad gauge line to Maiden Newton, on the 'main' Yeovil to Weymouth route. The line opened to the public on 12th November 1857 and was converted to standard gauge in June 1874. An extension to West Bay (1½ miles from Bridport) was brought into use on 31st March 1884. The extension was closed during the First World War as an economy measure and suffered permanent withdrawal of its passenger trains in September 1930. The final goods train operated to West Bay in 1962, but the last working of all was a special passenger train in August 1963. The Bridport branch was worked by auto trains from the 1930s and was dieselised in 1959, the engine shed at Bridport being closed from the same time. BR tried to shut the line in the 1960s, but narrow roads in the area were deemed unfit for buses and the branch survived until 3rd May 1975, by which time road improvements had presumably been undertaken.

Ken Wightman

Along the quay at Weymouth

The Weymouth quay line was authorised by the Weymouth & Portland Railway Act in 1862 and was brought into use in 1865. Initially dual gauge, it was worked by horses owned by the GWR until around 1880, when 'iron horses' took over. GWR 1366 Class 0-6-0PTs were normally used on the boat trains along the streets of Weymouth from the station to the quay. Here, No.1366 is seen moving gingerly along the 'tramway' with a boat train in the late 1950s. Note the vast number of people bathing in the sea and lying on the beach. Who needs Sitges or Corfu when one can enjoy a lovely warm summer's day on a spotlessly clean British beach rounded off with a fish and chip supper and a trip to the pub? Happy days!

Ken Wightman

After the Second World War holidays with pay became the norm for the masses, and in the 1950s there was an enormous growth in family holidays at a traditional British seaside resort. Car ownership was not yet as widespread as it is today, so the vast majority of families travelled by train, usually at the weekend during the peak months of July and August. In those days a holiday on the Channel Islands was probably regarded as really special, and one of the most popular routes was by train from Paddington which connected with a ferry from Weymouth. (The service switched to Waterloo from September 1959.) The boat trains ran along the streets of the town between Weymouth station and the quay, and latterly GWR 1366 Class 0-6-0PTs were employed on this work. When one of these locomotives was unavailable, Weymouth shed turned out a 5700 Class 0-6-0PT as evidenced here by this shot of No.7782 negotiating the quay with a trainload of returning holiday-makers on 4th July 1959.

Trevor Owen

Weymouth to Portland and Easton

A Railway Correspondence & Travel Society railtour, with 5700 Class pannier tank No.3737 in charge, pauses at the former Melcombe Regis station, on the Weymouth to Easton branch, on 14th August 1960. This line was authorised by the Weymouth & Portland Railway Act in 1862 as a dual gauge route and opened on 16th October 1865. Broad gauge working did not last long however, ceasing on 18th June 1874. The passenger service to Easton survived until 2nd March 1952, although Melcombe Regis station remained in use on Saturdays at the height of the summer season for some years afterwards. Freight trains continued to run on the line regularly until 1964, and then 'as required' until they ceased on 5th April 1965, but the last trip was actually made after this date to clear wagons. The branch was extremely scenic and offered fine vistas towards Portland Bill. The line also boasted a signalling system to warn of rock falls, similar to that used on the Oban line in Scotland. The signals were normally in the 'off' position, but when rocks fell onto the line, so disturbing the wires, the signals went to the 'on' position. The train seen here started at Waterloo behind SECR L Class 4-4-0 No.31768, an exile from the South Eastern Section, which gave way to T9 Class No.30718 at Salisbury, the latter powering the train to Weymouth via Yeovil (reverse). On the return trip from Easton to Weymouth there was some excitement, of a kind not normally experienced on RCTS tours, when the train was halted by police searching for escaped prisoners. Later in the day the participants returned to London via Fordingbridge, part of the journey back to the Capital being marred by torrential rain.

John Langford

Witham to Yatton

Draycott station, seen here on 9th June 1962, was one of a number of attractive stone-built wayside stations on the Witham to Yatton line. Note its most unusual Swiss chalet-style overhanging roof and tiny signal box. The station served a small village which nestles at the foot of the Mendip Hills. In the 1961 summer timetable a total of seven trains each way was advertised to run on weekdays between Yatton and Wells, while on Sundays the service was clearly designed for afternoon visitors to Wells. There was a single train from Yatton at 2.36pm which returned from Wells at 7.20pm. Good out and back connections were provided to and from Bristol.

Gerald Daniels

Left, above: The line from Witham to Yatton was not constructed as a single undertaking, but built by two entirely separate companies, the East Somerset Railway (ESR) and the Bristol & Exeter Railway (B&ER). The former constructed the line from Witham to Wells, while the latter built the section from Yatton to Wells. The first railway to be constructed in the Frome area was the Wiltshire, Somerset & Weymouth Railway which opened its line from Westbury to Frome on 7th October 1850. The ESR obtained its Act on 5th June 1856 for the stretch from Frome to Shepton Mallet, and in response to local pressure a Wells extension Act was passed a year later. The line opened to Shepton Mallet on 9th November 1858, an initial service of five weekday trains being provided. The extension to Wells was brought into use on 28th February 1862. The section from Yatton to Cheddar opened on 3rd August 1869, the stretch on to Wells opening for business on 5th April 1870. In the mid-1870s both routes were acquired by the GWR and converted to standard gauge. A connection was installed at Wells which enabled through running between the two lines, which commenced in 1878. In this view the fireman of Ivatt LMS-designed 2-6-2T No.41308, hauling a train from Yatton to Witham, is seen exchanging the single line tokens with the Cheddar signalman on 9th June 1962. GWR pannier tank locomotive No.9615 waits in the other platform with a train in the opposite direction. *Gerald Daniels*

Left, below: Rural stations do not come much finer than this! Another shot taken at Cheddar, this time showing bunker-first Ivatt Class 2MT 2-6-2T No.41240 waiting at the west end of the station on a lovely day in May 1960. The escarpment of the Mendip Hills is just visible in the background. During the late 1950s and early 1960s a number of these engines were allocated to the Western Region, and some were based in the Bristol division for the type of branch line duty seen here. Closure came for this scenic line on 9th September 1963, when the passenger trains ran for the last time. Freight trains continued from Yatton to Cheddar until 1st October 1964. *R. E. Toop*

Pictured with Cheddar Wood, and the slopes of the Mendip Hills in the background, BR Standard Class 3MT 2-6-2T No.82035 rolls into Axbridge with a two-coach train from Witham to Yatton on 11th May 1963. This was clearly a lovely, well-kept rural station in a perfect setting, but the dearth of passengers is an ominous sign for the future. Many of the pictures in this album feature GWR locomotive types, but here this relatively modern machine is an exception. This class was designed at Swindon Works however, so GWR aficionados would probably argue with justification that it is not entirely alien on this line.

J. Spencer Gilks

Yeovil to Taunton

The line from Taunton joined the Weymouth to Westbury line immediately south of Yeovil (Pen Mill) station, and the junction is seen here on 13th June 1958 with a GWR 2-6-2T tank locomotive approaching Pen Mill station, which is on the other side of a roadbridge behind the photographer. The tracks on the right led to Yeovil Town, which had a direct connection to the LSWR's Yeovil Junction station, and was a joint LSWR/GWR station. The tracks on the left are those to Dorchester and Weymouth, a line which is still open, albeit reduced to a single track following rationalisation undertaken in May/June 1968. Note the generous formation, indicating that both of these routes were originally built to broad gauge width. The diminutive Pen Mill shed is in the 'vee' formed by the Weymouth and Taunton lines. *Trevor Owen*

Right, above: The 1.23pm Saturday only train from Langport West to Yeovil, seen here awaiting departure from Langport West on 24th June 1961, was one of those workings which was a source of endless fascination to railway enthusiasts, but incredibly frustrating for *bona fide* travellers who simply wanted to arrive at their destination with a minimum of fuss. This train was formed with the locomotive and coaches off the 12.35pm from Taunton, which ran non-stop as far as Langport West, arriving at 12.55pm. When it reached the latter point however, the train waited for 28 minutes before resuming its journey to Yeovil, so was hardly designed for passengers in a hurry! The delay was doubtless due to the single line ahead being occupied by the 12.38pm SO from Yeovil (Pen Mill), but that reached Langport at 1.11pm, so it is a mystery why the 12.35pm had to wait until 1.23pm before resuming its journey. When the Westbury to Taunton 'cut off' line was commissioned in 1906 that joined the Yeovil line at Langport, where a station was built. This was known as Langport (East) while the existing station on the Yeovil line became Langport (West).   *John Langford*

Right, below: The railway from Taunton to Yeovil was authorised by an Act of Parliament in 1845 when the Bristol & Exeter Railway was authorised to construct a single track, broad gauge line from Durston Junction, on the main Taunton to Bristol route, to Hendford (Yeovil). At that time the only route from the West Country to London was via Bristol. The Taunton to Westbury line was not built until many years later. Work on the Yeovil line commenced in 1847, and the works had reached Martock by 1849, but were suspended for five years due to the B&ER giving priority to other projects. Construction was resumed in 1852 and the line opened in October 1853. On 2nd February 1857 an extension was opened to Yeovil (Pen Mill) to connect with the Westbury to Weymouth route. The Taunton to Yeovil line was converted to standard gauge in 1879. Like so many rural lines in the West Country, the Taunton to Yeovil route fell victim to the growth in private car ownership after the Second World War and after years of dwindling traffic, it was closed in June 1964. Here, BR Standard Class 3MT 2-6-2T No.82001 runs into Martock station with a Yeovil to Taunton train on 30th May 1964, just a few weeks prior to closure.   *Trevor Owen*

Yatton to Clevedon

The Bristol & Exeter Railway was authorised on 31st July 1845 to build the 3½ miles long broad gauge branch from Clevedon Road station (later Yatton), on the Bristol to Taunton line, to Clevedon. Construction was straightforward and the line opened on 28th July 1847. It was recorded that 2,000 passengers were carried on the first day and the Chairman and Directors of the B&ER were invited to a public breakfast at the Royal Hotel. The line was converted to standard gauge in 1879. The Clevedon trains used a bay at the west end of Yatton station's up platform. In the late 1950s a very frequent service was provided on the branch, a total of 31 down trains and 32 in the up direction being run on weekdays, the first train from Yatton being a goods working conveying passenger carriages which formed the first up train of the day. There was no Sunday service during the winter months. The line was operated under the 'one engine in steam' principle, usually by an auto train. There was a connection at Clevedon with the Weston, Clevedon & Portishead Light Railway, an outpost of the Colonel Stephens empire, until this was shut on 18th May 1940. The Clevedon line was closed by BR on 3rd October 1966 and a supermarket now occupies the Clevedon station site. In this portrait 1400 Class 0-4-2T No.1454 is captured taking water at Yatton on 28th April 1957. Note the small overall roof designed to protect passengers from the elements – the railway certainly seemed to look after travellers in those days. Judging by the gentlemen on the platform, most of whom appear to be railway buffs, the train in the other platform may have been an enthusiast's special. *Trevor Owen*

Chard to Taunton

There were various incredibly ambitious schemes in the 1840s for lines linking the Bristol and English channels – one was for a Watchet to Bridport route – and most of these were routed close to Chard or Ilminster. Not surprisingly, nothing came of these ideas and the first railway to serve Chard was a branch from Chard Road (later Chard Junction), on the LSWR's Yeovil to Exeter line, which was authorised by an Act of 25th May 1860. The line, brought into use on 8th May 1863, served Chard Town station on the eastern edge of the town which was described at the time as being 'close to Mr Heck's farmyard'. In 1861 the Chard & Taunton Railway obtained an Act of Parliament for a link between the towns, but owing to financial problems this company was taken over in 1863 by the Bristol & Exeter Railway who opened their broad gauge line from Chard to Taunton in September 1866. This line became one of the last broad gauge

branches, not being converted until 1891. The B&ER station was also served by the LSWR which installed a connecting spur between the two routes; the B&ER premises were known as 'Chard Joint', and for a short time was served by both gauges. The LSWR's Chard Town station was closed to passengers in 1916 and the GWR, successors to the B&ER, took over operation of the entire line to Chard Junction from 1st January 1917. Chard Joint station was renamed Chard Central in 1949, but by this time traffic had dwindled as a result of road competition. During the line's closing years, the weekday service consisted of only four trains in each direction, with additional workings between Chard Central and Junction stations. The fine B&ER station survived until the end, and in this shot 5700 Class 0-6-0PT No.5798 is seen at the south end of Central station after arrival with a train from Taunton on 13th June 1958.

Trevor Owen

A picture of the layout at the northern approach to Chard Central station, seen on 18th June 1960. There was only one through platform line, on the right, the track on the left served a bay platform. In the long-gone days when the station was served by two gauges, the broad gauge trains used the bay at the Taunton end of the premises while services from Chard Road ran into the southernmost bay, thus keeping the two as separate as possible. Both companies had sidings to a canal basin, situated just north of the station, and to reach this the LSWR used a dual gauge track which ran through the station. The Southern Region took control of the complete route on 2nd April 1950 although, curiously, the Western Region remained responsible for operation. It reverted to WR control in 1958. An ominous sign for the future was the temporary withdrawal of passenger trains in early 1951 due to a fuel crisis. This caused an outcry which resulted in trains being reinstated three months later. Surprisingly perhaps, trains continued to operate for a further eleven years, permanent withdrawal taking place from 10th September 1962. Right to the end passengers, at Chard Central were reminded of the line's ancestry by the words 'Bristol & Exeter Railway Booking Office' emblazoned over a doorway.

Roy Denison

Photographed just a few weeks before passenger services were withdrawn, GWR 5700 Class 0-6-0PT No.4622 is illustrated leaving Ilminster with the 4.30pm train from Taunton to Chard. This picture was taken on a sunny 18th August 1962. The layout here consisted of a single platformed station and a goods passing loop. The original Bristol & Exeter station buildings, which are partially visible in the background, lasted until closure. The last passenger train to serve Ilminster was the 9.30pm from Chard Junction to Taunton, hauled by pannier tank engine No.4663, on 8th September 1962. Goods traffic continued here for some time after closure to passengers (note the wagons in the yard) and was not withdrawn until 6th July 1964.

Alan Chandler

The Minehead Branch

The original West Somerset Railway was promoted locally and obtained an Act of Parliament in 1857 for a branch line from Norton Fitzwarren, near Taunton on the Bristol & Exeter Railway, to Watchet. This single track, broad gauge line was opened on 31st March 1862. In 1871 the line was extended from Watchet to Minehead (also broad gauge) by the Minehead Railway Company, which opened on 16th July 1874. The entire route was worked from the start by the B&ER, which was later acquired by the GWR, and the line was converted to standard gauge in 1882. Only a meagre passenger service was provided for many years, but by the 1930s the GWR had developed the holiday traffic potential and this continued after World War Two when the line was under BR Western Region jurisdiction. There were even through summer Saturday holiday trains from Paddington, Wolverhampton, Bristol and Cardiff, but they did not survive the Beeching cutbacks of the early 1960s, and the line fell into decline. It was closed by BR on 4th January 1971, but that was not the end for this attractive route. The West Somerset Railway Association was formed to save the branch, and with the co-operation of the local authority reopened part of the line in 1976. The line has gone through some difficult periods since reopening, but in recent years has emerged to become one of the foremost preserved lines in the country. So, thanks to the sterling efforts of many dedicated people, it is still possible to travel over the stretch of line seen here. GWR 2-6-2T No.4103 is depicted near Watchet hauling a Minehead-bound train on 10th June 1962.

Gerald Daniels

Right, above: Blue Anchor station is seen in this illustration which was taken on 6th August 1961. Thanks to the efforts of the West Somerset Railway (WSR), this station, and many others on this outstanding line, has been preserved for future generations to enjoy and savour the special magic of branch line travel, just as it was in steam days. When services resumed along the line in 1976 Blue Anchor (3½ miles from Minehead) was the limit of operations for a while, but trains now run as far as Bishop's Lydeard (19¾ miles) and the WSR can justifiably boast to be the longest preserved line in Great Britain. *Roy Denison*

Right, below: An unidentified GWR 2-6-2T locomotive leaves Blue Anchor with the 1.40pm Taunton to Minehead train also on 6th August 1961. The photographer was fortunate that the train's departure coincided with a shaft of sunlight on what appears to have been an otherwise fairly cloudy day. Blue Anchor station is adjacent to the beach, as evidenced by the parked cars and beach huts. The station was also noteworthy for a couple of camping coaches berthed in the sidings, other similar coaches being provided at Stogumber, down the line towards Taunton. *Roy Denison*

Taunton to Barnstaple

Milverton was the first station on the branch after Taunton and was conveniently sited for the village. The section between Milverton and Norton Fitzwarren was doubled by the GWR in 1937 to cater for increasing holiday traffic. The station retained its original B&ER buildings and had the undoubted luxury of gas lighting. In the early 1960s passengers from Milverton had a choice of six Monday to Friday trains in each direction, and this number also operated on Saturdays during the winter. In the peak summer months however, the line took on a different character with through services to Ilfracombe from places such as London, Wolverhampton and Manchester. Unlike the local trains, these were 'fast' trains and only called at the line's principal stations. After a very busy summer Saturday, in complete contrast the line always took a rest on Sundays – there was no Sunday service at any time of year. This picture was taken on 15th June 1963.

Gerald Daniels

Photographed against an attractive backdrop of rolling Devon hills, a train from Taunton to Barnstaple enters Dulverton station behind commendably clean 4300 Class 2-6-0 No.6337 on 5th August 1961. Note the fine selection of GWR signals and single line token equipment, all apparently newly repainted. The train pictured here is actually in Somerset, but the hills are across the county boundary in Devon, the River Exe forming the border at this point. Dulverton was one of the few centres of population on this line, but the station could not be described as conveniently sited in relation to the village. Passengers for the village without their own transport were faced with the choice of waiting for a taxi or a 2¼ miles-long walk, so they had to be really determined travellers.

Roy Denison

A delightful study of GWR Collett 2251 Class 0-6-0 No.3205 passing Filleigh, between Barnstaple and Dulverton, on 27th March 1965 with 'The Exmoor Ranger' railtour. The train is heading eastwards towards Taunton. During the course of the day participants had travelled over the Halwill Junction to Torrington line, part of which had been officially closed to all traffic some weeks previously, and special permission had to be obtained to traverse this scenic byway. Later the train visited Ilfracombe and it returned to Barnstaple before taking participants on to Taunton. This must have been a wonderful day out and one, sadly, that is not repeatable today. Most of the routes used by the train seen here have long since been closed and the track lifted.

Roy Hobbs

The 44¾ miles-long line from Taunton to Barnstaple, which skirts the southern slopes of Exmoor, is undoubtedly one of the most picturesque featured in this album. The Devon & Somerset Railway was authorised in the session of 1864 to construct a broad gauge line from Barnstaple to a junction with the Bristol & Exeter Railway, near Taunton. Work started in the following year, but progress was slow and by the summer of 1871 only the first 7¼ miles from Watchet Junction (now Norton Fitzwarren) to Wiveliscombe had been finished. This short section opened on 8th June of that year. The route was opened throughout to Barnstaple on 1st November 1873. The line was converted to standard gauge in 1881. A connection between the GWR (which had absorbed the B&ER in 1877) and the LSWR was constructed at Barnstaple, and opened in 1887. At first, trains from the GWR on to LSWR tracks had to reverse in Barnstaple GWR station, but in 1905 a curve was laid which permitted direct running into the LSWR's Barnstaple Junction station. After nationalisation the GWR station was renamed 'Barnstaple Victoria Road' to distinguish it from the town's other stations, but on 13th June 1960 it was closed and trains were diverted to the junction station. In this shot, the same railtour seen in the previous picture is at the former Victoria Road station in March 1965, by which time the premises, which were still being used for goods traffic, were looking rather dilapidated. The locomotives are LMSR-designed Ivatt 2-6-2Ts, Nos.41206 and 41291.

Roy Hobbs

The Hemyock Branch

Small's Seeds may very well have succeeded and the delightful Hemyock branch also succeeded, providing both passenger and goods transport for the residents of the Culm Valley for almost a century. This 7½ miles-long line, which had an immense character all of its own, was authorised in 1873 as a single track, standard gauge light railway and opened on 29th May 1876. The line followed the sinuous course of the River Culm and, as if this natural feature did not create enough severe curvature, it was also forced around even tighter curves in order to avoid fields belonging to landowners who had opposed the building of the line! Passenger, mixed and milk trains were operated and these were restricted to an overall 15mph speed limit. It was the fireman's duty to open and close crossing gates at various points on the line. Prior to closure to passenger traffic, which occurred on 9th September 1963, three trains from Tiverton Junction to Hemyock were advertised on weekdays and four in the reverse direction. There was also an additional service about mid-day which ran to Uffculme only. There were no passenger trains on Sundays. Here, bunker-first 1400 Class 0-4-2T No.1451 is depicted leaving Uffculme with a train bound for Tiverton Junction on 7th August 1961.   *Roy Denison*

A view of Culmstock station with No. 1451 waiting in the platform at the head of a mixed train bound for Hemyock. Note the milk tanks on the rear of the train. This picture was also taken on 7th August 1961. The coach is a former Barry Railway gaslit vehicle, one of two carriages (Nos. W263W and W268W) which at the time were the only passenger coaches permitted over the line due to its tight curves. These vehicles were a great attraction to railway enthusiasts and at the time of their withdrawal had become the last gaslit carriages on the Western Region. The line's profitable milk traffic was probably the main reason why this rural backwater survived for so long. The importance of this traffic can be gauged by the fact that milk trains even ran on Sundays in order to ensure fresh supplies.

Roy Denison

Branch line scenes do not come more placid than this! Photographed on 5th August 1963, just over a month before passenger trains ran for the last time, 1400 Class 0-4-2T No.1451 is depicted shunting in the delightful and peaceful setting of Hemyock station. The engine is apparently propelling its one-coach train out of the platform prior to running-round, there being no loop line adjacent to the platform. The waters of the infant River Culm are in the foreground. On the last day of services, trains were in charge of sister locomotive No.1421, which was in commendably clean condition, and formed of two *ex*-LNER short wheelbase Thompson-designed brake second coaches, Nos.W87270E and W87245E. The latter had been drafted in to replace the aged *ex*-Barry Railway vehicles during the previous year. Apart from a fair sized crowd which gathered at Hemyock to witness the departure of the last train, there was reportedly little interest shown in the closure, as local folk in this thinly populated valley had long since deserted the railway for other forms of transport. The line was closed completely on 3rd November 1975.   *Michael Allen*

The Exe Valley Line

The 1.45pm train from Tiverton to Exeter which is being propelled by an unknown 1400 Class 0-4-2T locomotive, stands in Thorverton station on a rather dull day, 15th June 1963. The goods yard appears to be reasonably busy, with a horsebox standing in front of the cattle dock and a fair number of wagons litter the yard. Note the vintage hand crane. There was a mill at Thorverton which used to produce considerable railway traffic; it was connected to the branch by a siding which was laid in 1898. Following withdrawal of the passenger service in 1963, the section from Stoke Canon, on the main Exeter to Taunton line, to Thorverton was retained for goods traffic until 30th November 1966.

Gerald Daniels

Tiverton station on 18th July 1964, after the withdrawal of the Exe Valley trains. Well, how is that for a day out? 'Sunday by the Sea' at either Exmouth or Sidmouth for a very reasonable bargain fare! Let us hope that the trippers picked a nice, warm day and had a really lovely time at the seaside. The Western Region's local advertising does not appear to have been very sophisticated by today's standards, but at least they were trying to drum up some much-needed business for the railway, which was most commendable, but far too late to save the line from oblivion. Note the station furniture which had doubtless hardly changed from the day the line opened in 1848 – enamel signs, wooden platform barrows and seats plus, of course, the stone-built station building. Perhaps the blackboard should have implored 'Book your seats for Sidmouth now, this is your last chance, Beeching is closing the line in three months time'.

Roy Denison

A charming, everyday platform-end scene at Tiverton on 22nd August 1959 as members of the station staff chat to the crew of an unidentified 1400 Class 0-4-2T prior to departure to Tiverton Junction with an auto train working. Note the traditional gas lighting and wooden platform trolley. The local bus garage evidently adjoined the station and two vehicles, which today would be regarded as museum pieces, are visible behind the engine. The first railway to reach the town was the broad gauge branch from Tiverton Junction, opened on 12th June 1848. The next line to be planned was that from Stoke Canon, just north of Exeter, to Tiverton this section being authorised in June 1874. Construction was considerably delayed and protracted however, and the section northwards from Tiverton to Morebath Junction, which had been promoted in 1875 as the Tiverton and North Devon Railway, was the first to be completed. This opened on 1st August 1884 while the opening of the line below Tiverton was delayed until 1st May 1885. The line from Tiverton Junction was converted to standard gauge in June 1884, in preparation for the opening of the Exe Valley line from Morebath Junction. *Alan Jarvis*

The Moretonhampstead Branch

The 12¼ miles-long broad gauge branch line from Newton Abbot to Moretonhampstead was opened on 4th July 1866 under an Act promoted by the Moretonhampstead & South Devon Railway Company and passed in 1862. The line was worked from the start by the South Devon Railway, which absorbed the local company in 1872. The station seen here is Heathfield, previously known as Chudleigh Road, which was brought into use in 1874. The change of name dates from 1882 when the Teign Valley Railway was opened from Heathfield to Ashton, with a goods only extension to Christow. The Teign Valley line was built as a standard gauge route and was isolated from the rest of the system until gauge conversion of the Moretonhampstead line occurred in 1892. For a while Heathfield station was an interchange point between the broad and standard gauge tracks. When this portrait of Heathfield station was recorded on 5th March 1961 the passenger train service had been withdrawn for some time, but the station appears to be in an excellent state of repair with all of the signalling apparently intact.

John Langford

This picture of 5700 Class 0-6-0PT No.3600 running round its one-coach train at Moretonhampstead on 15th September 1958 has a lovely remote and peaceful feeling. The timber-roofed station building is visible on the left. Unfortunately, from the travellers' point of view, this spot became even more remote when passenger services were withdrawn from 2nd March 1959. The last services actually operated on Saturday 28th February 1959, when 1400 Class 0-4-2T No.1466 was noted hauling trains which had been specially strengthened to three-coach formations. In GWR days nine weekday and two Sunday trains were generally advertised, the service when the line closed being seven weekday trains. The line reached an altitude of 588ft above sea level and had some fierce gradients, such as the 1 in 53 between Pullabrook Halt and Lustleigh and even steeper 1 in 49 climb into Moretonhampstead station. At one time the GWR ran connecting buses from there to Chagford, which competed with the LSWR road service from Exeter to Chagford. *Trevor Owen*

Paignton to Kingswear

The short, two miles-long branch from Churston, on the Paignton to Kingswear line, to the small fishing port of Brixham could hardly be described as the most interesting branch line in Devon. Its shortness and lack of any intermediate stopping place were decided drawbacks, a further factor being the absence of any signalling, apart from one or two at the Churston end, because the route was worked on the 'one engine in steam' principle. A local resident promoted the Torbay & Brixham Railway which was authorised on 25th June 1864 and the line opened on 28th February 1868. The terminus, which had a very cramped layout, was inconveniently sited on the hillside above the town and this must have deterred all but the most determined traveller. Despite this disadvantage, the weekdays only passenger service was quite frequent; goods traffic was handled by a mixed train. This unremarkable line was closed completely on 13th May 1963. In this study, 1400 Class 0-4-2T No.1470 is seen at Churston awaiting departure with an auto train working on 18th July 1958. *Trevor Owen*

It is arguable whether the Paignton to Kingswear line qualifies for inclusion in a book devoted solely to former GWR South West branch lines. Certainly, in BR days, this heavily-graded single track route, with its delightful terminus situated on the east bank of the River Dart, had all the atmosphere of a branch railway and, during the dreary winter months, also a train service more appropriate to a branch line. On summer Saturdays in the 1950s and 1960s however, the timetable told a much different story. Through trains conveying restaurant facilities were scheduled to Birmingham, Bradford, Manchester and, of course, London Paddington. Passengers for London could travel on the famous 'Torbay Express' which served the Kingswear branch and, in the summer 1961 timetable, was advertised to run non-stop between Torquay and Paddington in 4hr. 10min. Even on Mondays to Fridays through main line services were provided. The line's historical background is straightforward. The South Devon Railway had opened to Torquay (Torre) in December 1848, and the Dartmouth & Torbay Railway was incorporated in 1857 to extend the branch. The section onwards to

Paignton was opened on 2nd August 1859, the next stretch to Churston started in business on 14th March 1861, with the final link to Kingswear opening on 16th August 1864. The area occupied by Kingswear station and the fairly extensive carriage sidings was built on land reclaimed from the River Dart. A curious feature of the Kingswear branch was Dartmouth 'station', on the opposite bank of the river. Dartmouth was not rail-served, but nonetheless appeared in the public timetable, passengers being advised to use 'the British Railways ferry to Kingswear'. In 1972, when BR's plans to close the Paignton to Kingswear line were made public, the Devon County Council subsidised the service until it was taken over by a private operator. So, at least in the summertime, the confident bark of a GWR steam engine still echoes around the beautiful countryside in this part of glorious Devon. Here, in this scene recorded in the early 1960s, 6100 Class 2-6-2T No.6146 is depicted at Kingswear against a magnificent background of wooded hills and the river.

R. E. Toop

The Kingsbridge Branch

Left, above: Kingsbridge station was, perhaps, the archetypal GWR branch line terminal station which must have been replicated on many a railway modeller's layout. The passenger facilities consisted of a long curving platform with a bay; the stone-built station building had a platform canopy. The goods yard had four sidings, cattle pens and a stone-built goods shed. In addition, there was a modest carriage shed, part of which is just visible on the extreme left of this illustration, and an engine shed, which is on the right. In the late 1950s seven trains were scheduled on Mondays to Fridays in both directions, with an eighth up train on Saturdays only. Some of the trains were designated as 'mixed'. There was no Sunday service. In June 1961 diesel railcars replaced steam traction on the branch trains, while North British Type 2 1100hp diesel-hydraulics ventured down to Kingsbridge on the through summer workings to and from London. The end for this lovely line came, amidst much public outcry, on 16th September 1963.   *Trevor Owen*

Left, below: The South Devon Railway's extension westwards from Totnes to Laira was completed by 5th May 1848, but the branch line from Brent to Kingsbridge arrived on the scene much later. Proposals had been put forward by the Kingsbridge Railway Company in 1864, but insufficient capital was raised. In 1882 the Kingsbridge & Salcombe Railway Act was passed, but its powers were transferred to the GWR who raised the necessary monies under their New Lines Act of 13th August 1888. The single-track standard-gauge route was opened to Kingsbridge on 19th December 1893, early plans to serve Salcombe by rail having been overtaken by the GWR's growing network of bus services which fed railheads throughout the system. A bus service from Salcombe to Kingsbridge commenced in July 1909. There were three intermediate stations on the branch. Trains leaving Kingsbridge were faced with a two miles-long climb, mostly at 1 in 50, to a point between the Kingsbridge estuary and the River Avon, the course of which the line follows for most of the way. In this shot 4575 Class 2-6-2T No.5525, hauling a Brent-bound train, bustles up towards the 625 yards-long Sorely Tunnel, the only major engineering work on the line, in which the summit was located. So, it cannot be said that the locomotive's crew have the summit in their sights!

R. E. Toop

Plymouth to Launceston

Yelverton station, and a two-coach Launceston to Plymouth train, are the subject of this illustration. Yelverton, situated between Tavistock and Plymouth, is best known as the junction for the former branch to Princetown, which is situated on bleak, inhospitable moorland 1,373ft. above sea level. This line was closed completely by BR on 5th March 1956, from which date Yelverton lost its junction status. The train is the 10.15am from Launceston, headed by 4575 Class 2-6-2T No.4588, and this picture was taken in February 1962. This section of the Launceston branch (south of Tavistock) was promoted by the Tavistock & South Devon Railway who obtained an Act in July 1854 and the line was opened in June 1859 when two special trains ran non-stop from Plymouth, apparently completing the 16 miles-long journey in 37 minutes.

Peter Gray/Colour-Rail

Left, above: The largest intermediate settlement on the Launceston branch was Tavistock, where the former GWR station was known latterly as 'Tavistock South'. This station boasted a most impressive and distinctive overall roof which spanned three tracks. In this picture the 10.15am Launceston to Plymouth is seen again, this time on 15th September 1962 with 2-6-2T No.4591 running bunker-first, waiting under the roof before resuming its journey to Plymouth. The last day of passenger operation was 29th December 1962, a day some railway enthusiasts who decided to make a last trip along the branch will remember for altogether different reasons. During that afternoon heavy snow started to fall which soon developed into a blizzard. The last booked passenger trains from both Plymouth and Launceston were cancelled due to the severe weather conditions and the 6.20pm *ex*-Plymouth travelled no further than Tavistock. In the reverse direction the 7.10pm from Tavistock to Plymouth, which had some enthusiasts aboard, became marooned in the snow at Bickleigh and it was the following morning before they, and the other passengers, were able to reach home.
Michael Allen

Left, below: The location is Lydford, 600 feet above sea level on the western fringe of Dartmoor. There are actually two stations here, the LSWR's being on the left while the GWR's premises are on the right. This explains the substantial layout, which was a legacy of competition between these rival companies, and was quite disproportionate to the amount of traffic on offer, Lydford being little more than a village. Even in the late 1950s the train service on the SR's 'main' Plymouth to Exeter line was not generous, Lydford being served by only seven weekday trains on that route, in addition to a smaller number on the Launceston branch. The first railway to reach here was the South Devon Railway's broad gauge line from Tavistock which opened on 1st July 1865. The LSWR's extension from Okehampton arrived on the scene in October 1874 and continued to Plymouth using the South Devon's tracks, which were converted to dual gauge. On 2nd June 1890 the LSWR obtained its own separate route to Plymouth with the opening of the Plymouth, Devonport & South Western Junction Railway's line, which was subsequently acquired by the LSWR. Lydford signal box had the distinction of two separate frames – one for each of the original companies. Churchward 2-6-2T No.4591 (again!) was photographed leaving Lydford with a Launceston train on 18th June 1958.
Trevor Owen

Yes, its No.4591 yet again, this time standing at Launceston after arrival with the 7.10am from Plymouth on 15th September 1962, a miserable, damp day. Perhaps this locomotive's principal claim to fame is that it was the most photographed engine on the Launceston branch – quite an accolade! The top section of the Launceston branch above Tavistock was opened, as previously mentioned, on 1st July 1865. Trains on the GWR line had their own terminus, Launceston (North) station, but this was relegated to goods-only status from 30th June 1952, from which date services used the LSWR station, as seen here. When passenger trains to and from Plymouth were withdrawn from 31st December 1962, the sections between Launceston and Lifton, plus the line south of Tavistock were closed completely, but a goods service was retained to Lifton to serve an Ambrosia milk factory. Access to Lifton was achieved by running a daily goods train from Okehampton via Lydford, where there was a connection between the LSWR and GWR routes. This train in addition served Tavistock, which also kept its goods facilities for a while after its passengers trains ceased. The latter place lost its goods trains from 7th September 1964, while those to Lifton lasted until 28th February 1966. Launceston continued to be served by trains on the Exeter-Okehampton-Wadebridge line until 3rd October 1966.   *Michael Allen*

Liskeard to Looe

The history of the 8¾ miles-long branch from Liskeard to Looe is quite fascinating and can be traced back to 28th November 1844 when the Liskeard & Caradon Railway started in business, conveying granite and copper ore from Caradon to the canal basin at Moorswater. This line was built to standard gauge, the flat bottom rails being laid on granite blocks. The Liskeard & Looe Union canal, which dated from 1828, was used to convey the minerals from Moorswater but when traffic reached 40,000 tons annually the canal company extended the line to Looe and the the Liskeard & Looe Railway was created. This opened to goods traffic, amidst the usual local celebrations, on 27th December 1860. People were conveyed in open goods wagons, there being no passenger stock until the line commenced passenger operations on 11th September 1879. There was no connection from the main line until the GWR installed a loop from Liskeard in May 1901. The branch platform there was at right angles to the main line and this connection, which descended on a rather spectacular spiralling course, met the branch at Coombe Junction, where reversal was necessary. The GWR took over the Looe branch in 1909. In this charming view 4575 Class 2-6-2T No.5539 is seen waiting at Coombe Junction with a train to Looe on 12th August 1960. Moorswater viaduct, which carries the main line west of Liskeard, towers above the valley in the background.

Roy Denison

Trains between Liskeard and Looe, as previously mentioned, have to reverse at Coombe Junction which, even with today's uninspiring diesel multiple units, is still an interesting and quite unusual operation. In the age of steam this manoeuvre was more time consuming, and was achieved by the locomotive noisily running round its train. The operation was usually carried out in an extremely slick manner – after all most of the engine crews and guards had years of practice. In this scene, recorded on 19th July 1958, 4575 class tank engine No.4584 is seen attacking the steep climb towards Liskeard station, its sharp bark no doubt echoing back off the surrounding hills. This photograph was taken from a conveniently situated roadbridge which carries the main Liskeard to Looe road across the railway at this point.

Trevor Owen

The railway line from Liskeard to Looe generally follows the course of the Looe River, which is little more than a small stream for most of the way. Just before the terminus it is joined by the West Looe River, the estuary dividing East and West Looe. 4575 Class tank engine No.4584 is seen again in this shot, which was taken looking across the water towards East Looe, where the railway is situated. Steam traction on this branch still had more than three years to run at the time of this photograph, diesel units taking over operations from the start of the winter 1961 timetable. The survival of this delightful backwater is apparently due to the unsuitability of some local roads for buses.

Trevor Owen

Bodmin Road to Bodmin General

Bodmin General was one of the most appealing stations in Cornwall, perhaps *the* most appealing, which had the atmosphere of a branch line terminal station, although in reality it was not actually the end of a line. It possessed a tiny engine shed, goods shed and dainty signal box, all crammed into a small area. It was a railway modeller's delight, and must have been replicated on many layouts up and down the country. The line on the extreme left is that from Wadebridge, the middle track being the 'main line' to Bodmin Road. No.4584 is seen easing away from the platform bunker-first with a Wadebridge train, while No.4569 waits in the siding adjacent to the tiny engine shed. Note the rhododendron bushes behind the signal post. *Trevor Owen*

A 'Southern' intruder at Bodmin General! Even though the locomotive may not be of Southern parentage, the Maunsell coaches indicate that this train had started somewhere on former Southern Region territory. In fact the train had just arrived after forming the 6.55am from Wadebridge on 1st June 1963. Note that the guard appears to have placed the tail lamp in position for the return trip before the LMSR Ivatt-designed 2-6-2T locomotive had been detached. This picture also illustrates the very restricted station site. Most trains from Wadebridge ran to Bodmin General and some continued to Bodmin Road for main line connections, but a handful terminated at Bodmin North, the former LSWR premises. All of these services ceased from 30th January 1967, but the line between (what is now) Bodmin Parkway and Bodmin General and beyond to Boscarne Junction is now operated by the Bodmin & Wenford Railway.   *Alan Chandler*

Lostwithiel to Fowey

The original broad gauge Lostwithiel & Fowey Railway was brought into use for goods traffic as far as Carne Point on 1st June 1869, but ran into financial difficulties and was closed from 1st January 1880. It was reopened as a standard gauge route by the GWR on 16th September 1895 and extended a short distance to link up with the former line from St. Blazey to Fowey. The St. Blazey to Fowey passenger trains ceased operation as long ago as 1929, but those from Lostwithiel to Fowey lasted until 4th January 1965. The area is well known for its deposits of china clay, much of which is exported through the port of Fowey, and in this view of Fowey station 5700 Class 0-6-0PT No.8702 is seen hauling a distinctive train of short wheelbase china clay wagons. On the left an auto train is forming a local working to Lostwithiel. This picture was taken on 15th October 1960.

John Langford

An unidentified 1400 Class 0-4-2T waits at the other end of Fowey station's platform with a train to Lostwithiel. This photograph was also taken on 15th October 1960. Note the neat and tidy station premises and attractive floral displays on the platform. In addition to the through platform seen here, there was also a short bay platform part of which is just discernible on the right. Fowey station was located in a rather picturesque setting almost surrounded by trees and more distant hills. *John Langford*

Par to Newquay

Right, above: A 5700 Class 0-6-0PT, No.7709, is shown at St. Blazey, just west of Par on the line to Newquay, with a china clay working on 4th May 1959. In many respects this line is the most interesting covered by this volume. The sections from St. Blazey to Bugle and from Newquay to St. Dennis, dating from 1842 and 1849 respectively, were pioneered by Squire Joseph Thomas Treffrey of Place, near Fowey, who was the landowner of much of this area in early Victorian days, and wanted transport for the vast mineral deposits on his estates. The former line, built to standard gauge, strode across the beautiful Luxulyan valley on a ten-arch 98ft. high, 216 yards-long granite viaduct, which took three years to build. This line also featured a cable-worked incline with a gradient of 1 in 10. In 1872 the Cornwall Minerals Railway was authorised to construct a through route from St. Blazey to Newquay using parts of the lines built by Treffrey and after feverish activity this opened in 1874, using a new formation up the western side of the Luxulyan valley which avoided the incline. But due to an economic depression the minerals line fell on hard times and in October 1877 the GWR took over. Two years later it opened a connection from its main line at Par to St. Blazey, but due to mixed gauges through working was not possible until 1892. *John Edgington*

Right, below: The Newquay branch has some fearsome gradients, notably the extremely stiff 1 in 40 climb from St. Blazey to Luxulyan and similar inclines in both directions to a summit near Roche. When 'holidays with pay' became the norm for the masses after the end of the Second World War there was a huge increase in summer holiday traffic to resorts in the south west of England, Newquay in particular being a favourite destination. During peak weekends in the late 1950s sometimes as many as a dozen heavy holiday trains were scheduled to leave Newquay between Friday evening and Saturday afternoon, and the working of these trains, most of which would require piloting or banking assistance, was something of a headache for the operating authorities. The 'Kings' and 4700 Class 2-8-0s were not allowed on the Newquay branch (indeed, they were prohibited west of Plymouth), but other main line classes, including large locomotives such as 'Castles', were permitted, and were by no means uncommon. Those machines were restricted to 230 tons unassisted up the bank towards Luxulyan, while the limit for a 'Hall' Class was 190 tons. In this view the 12.30pm SO Newquay to Paddington train, hauled by the powerful combination of Nos.7816 *Frilsham Manor* and 6801 *Aylburton Grange*, is seen crossing Goss Moor as it approaches Roche summit. The 'Grange' Class locomotive gained the unfortunate distinction of being the first of its class to be condemned, which occurred in November 1960. This portrait was recorded on 13th September 1958. *Trevor Owen*

Today the Newquay branch is a pale shadow of the busy line of steam days and is largely reduced to 'basic railway' status. Here, Newquay station is seen in more prosperous times, albeit outside the summer period, with 4575 Class 2-6-2T No.4593 sitting near the buffer stops after arrival with the 10.20am local train from Par. This train appears to have operated as a 'mixed', note the open wagon and 'vanfit' on the rear, which are apparently being shunted off by a pannier tank engine. Newquay station had three extremely long platforms, the ends of which are almost, but not quite, out of camera range. No.4593 certainly earned its keep on the day of this photograph, because no sooner had it arrived at Newquay (due 11.21am), it was on its way to Chacewater at the head of the 11.50am stopping train.   *John Langford*

Newquay to Chacewater

Many of the lines illustrated in this volume were initially planned by purely local companies, but the 18½ miles-long Chacewater to Newquay line was an exception. It was the final passenger line to be built in Cornwall and the first section from Chacewater to Perranporth was opened by the GWR on 6th July 1903. The remaining stretch of the route, from Perranporth to Newquay carried its first passengers on 2nd January 1905. Construction of this line thwarted any territorial ambitions the LSWR may have had in this part of Cornwall. Some of the stations on the route had an unusual island platform layout, an example being Perranporth, the principal station on the line, which was photographed on 7th August 1960 with No.5564 waiting in the platform with a train to Newquay. The line was also noted for its profusion of GWR halts with 'Pagoda' style waiting shelters, in fact most of the stations on the route were halts, there being only three proper stations. This route had considerable individual character, so it is a great pity it was closed in February 1963.

Roy Denison

A train to Newquay is seen leaving Shepherds station behind 4575 Class 2-6-2T No.4587 in September 1958. Note the clerestory coach tucked away in the siding. This was the only crossing station on the Chacewater to Newquay line to have conventional side platforms. There was no footbridge at Shepherds and passengers alighting there had to cross the tracks. The section between Shepherds and Newquay followed the course of an old mineral line, the first section of which was opened in 1849 from Newquay to East Wheal Rose mine, Newlyn East. This line was firstly extended to Treamble and later to Gravel Hill, though the latter stretch only lasted until 1888. When the Perranporth to Newquay line opened for passenger traffic in 1905, Shepherds became the junction for the Treamble mineral branch which closed in 1917 only to be reopened in 1926! Services ceased in summer 1949, with official closure on 1st January 1952.

Trevor Owen/Colour-Rail

The St. Ives Branch

Right, above: The journey from St. Erth to St. Ives may be short, but at least memories of the branch's stunning coastline, smooth golden sand and deep blue sea crashing onto the rocks will linger long in the mind. This 4¼ miles-long line, the last to be built to the broad gauge, was opened on 1st June 1877. The short section as far as Lelant Quay was converted to mixed gauge in 1888 and four years later the broad gauge was abandoned. In this wonderfully panoramic shot of St. Ives Bay hundreds of happy holidaymakers can be seen either on the beach or frolicking in the surf while 4500 Class 2-6-2T No.4566 simmers in the station, presumably prior to returning to St. Erth with a passenger working. This picture was taken on 11th June 1961.   *Michael Allen*

Right, below: Another picture of No.4566 awaiting departure to St. Erth on the same day as the previous shot, this time showing part of the station building, signal box and track layout. In addition, note the camping coaches, and ivy-clad engine shed in the middle background. The official end of steam on the branch came on 9th September 1961, just three months after this scene was recorded, when the shed serviced its last locomotive.
Michael Allen

Oh dear, this time a picture taken on a rainy August day in 1960 at St. Ives, thus proving conclusively that even that favoured resort cannot guarantee sunshine all of the time! No.4566 (again!) stands in the long, curving platform with its four-coach train while a sister locomotive waits to take over at the other end. During the summer months an intensive service was operated on the branch for which three engines were rostered. These were essential in order to maintain the tight turn-rounds at each end of the line. On Saturdays there was a through train to Paddington, which (in the 1961 summer timetable) left St. Ives at 9.20am, and was often made up to ten coaches and double-headed. The down train from Paddington was 'The Cornish Riviera' which arrived here at 5.40pm. These were remarkable sights on the branch where a two-coach train more than sufficed for most of the year. In the early 1970s the layout and station facilities at St. Ives were drastically reduced in an economy drive.

Roy Denison